# FORGOTTEN
# CITIES

by Charlie Samuels

# Crabtree Publishing Company
www.crabtreebooks.com

# Crabtree Publishing Company
## www.crabtreebooks.com

**Author:** Charlie Samuels
**Project Coordinator:** Kathy Middleton
**Editors:** Molly Aloian, Tim Cooke
**Proofreader:** Crystal Sikkens
**Designer:** Lynne Lennon
**Cover Design:** Margaret Amy Salter
**Picture Researcher:** Andrew Webb
**Picture Manager:** Sophie Mortimer
**Art Director:** Jeni Child
**Editorial Director:** Lindsey Lowe
**Children's Publisher:** Anne O'Daly
**Production Coordinator and
    Prepress Technician:** Michael Golka
**Print Coordinator:** Katherine Berti

**Photographs**
**Cover: Thinkstock:** Hemera
**Interior: istockphoto:** 9b, 24; **Public Domain:** Jan Derk 25; **Robert Hunt Library:** 9t; **Shutterstock:** 4, 7t, 13, 16, 21, Mike von Bergen 23, Linda Bucklin 6, Roman Czupryniak 12, André Goncalves 17, Vladimir Korostyshevskiy 20, Opis 5, 18, Jarno Gonzalez Zarraonandia 22; **Thinkstock:** Digital Vision 15, Dorling Kindersley 10–11, 11t, Hemera 28, istockphoto 14, 19, 26–27, 27, 29, Photos.com 7b, 8.

**Library and Archives Canada Cataloguing in Publication**

Samuels, Charlie, 1961-
    Forgotten cities / Charlie Samuels.

(Mystery files)
Includes index.
Issued also in electronic formats.
ISBN 978-0-7787-8007-6 (bound).--ISBN 978-0-7787-8012-0 (pbk.).


    1. Extinct cities--Juvenile literature. 2. Civilization, Ancient--Juvenile literature. 3. Excavations (Archaeology)--Juvenile literature. I. Title. II. Series: Mystery files (St. Catharines, Ont.)

CC176.S26 2012          j930.1          C2012-906373-8

**Library of Congress Cataloging-in-Publication Data**

Samuels, Charlie, 1961-
    Forgotten cities / Charlie Samuels.
        p. cm. --  (Mystery files)
    Includes index.
    ISBN 978-0-7787-8007-6 (reinforced library binding : alk. paper) -- ISBN 978-0-7787-8012-0 (pbk. : alk. paper) -- ISBN 978-1-4271-9337-7 (electronic pdf) -- ISBN 978-1-4271-9325-4 (electronic html)
    1.  Extinct cities--Juvenile literature. 2.  Cities and towns, Ancient--Juvenile literature. 3.  Civilization, Ancient--Juvenile literature. 4.  Excavations (Archaeology)--Juvenile literature. I. Title.

CC176.S26 2013
930.1--dc23
                                                                2012037924

## Crabtree Publishing Company
www.crabtreebooks.com          1-800-387-7650

**Published in Canada**
**Crabtree Publishing**
616 Welland Ave.
St. Catharines, ON
L2M 5V6

**Published in the United States**
**Crabtree Publishing**
PMB 59051
350 Fifth Avenue, 59th Floor
New York, New York 10118

**Published by CRABTREE PUBLISHING COMPANY in 2013**
Copyright © 2013 Brown Bear Books Ltd

Printed in the U.S.A./112012/FA20121012

# Contents

Introduction 4

Mystery of ATLANTIS 6

The Mound of the DEAD 8

The City of MUD 10

Homer's TROY 12

The Buried ARMY 14

Victims of the VOLCANO 16

City of the ROCKS 18

Faces in the JUNGLE 20

Lost City of the INCA 22

Africa's Royal CITY 24

Pakal's Resting PLACE 26

City of the GODS 28

Glossary 30

Find Out More 31

Index 32

# Introduction

Babylon was once the most powerful city in the world. Today, its site is marked by piles of mud in the desert of Iraq. Around the world, dusty ruins are the only reminders of once flourishing, bustling cities that were crammed with thousands of people.

This book explores the mysteries of the world's forgotten cities, together with a lost continent, and a buried army of warriors. Why were they abandoned and how were they rediscovered?

Pompeii was buried by ash from a volcano for 1,700 years.

*The city of Petra, in Jordan, was carved into rocky cliffs.*

## Decline and Fall

Some of these cities were trade centers. Others were centers of political power or had religious significance. But they were all eventually abandoned and then forgotten. They were overgrown by the jungle or buried beneath sand or ash. Some ruins lay undisturbed in rocky canyons or high on mountain peaks.

This book will take you from China to the Andes Mountains of Peru and from India to ancient Italy. You will read the remarkable stories of forgotten cities, their rediscovery, and how **archaeologists** solved their mysteries.

Mystery words...

archaeologist: someone who studies objects from the past

# Mystery of
# ATLANTIS

Some people believe that the legendary island of Atlantis lies at the bottom of the Atlantic Ocean. According to the ancient Greek philosopher Plato, this lost civilization was once a paradise on Earth.

Ancient accounts say that Atlantis was a large island off the west coast of Europe. At its height, around 9600 B.C., it was a powerful civilization.

The cities of Atlantis were destroyed when the island sank.

Atlantis was said to be bigger than Asia, and its people were very wealthy and happy. But when the Athenians of Greece defeated the Atlanteans, the island fell into **anarchy**. The people of Atlantis became wicked and greedy for power. According to legend, a huge earthquake hit the island and Atlantis sank to the bottom of the Atlantic Ocean.

## Looking for Atlantis

Many people have looked for evidence that Atlantis once existed. No one has found any sign of it, even using high-tech tools like **sonar** to map the seabed. But there are still people who believe that the island once existed.

Some people say that Atlantis helped spread new ideas across the world. That might explain why, for example, pyramids were built by ancient peoples in both Egypt and Mexico.

Atlantis used to appear on some old maps of the Atlantic Ocean.

# The Mound of the DEAD

A huge dirt mound near the border of Pakistan and India had a mysterious name—Mohenjo-Daro, or the Mound of the Dead. Archaeologists first heard about the mound in the 1920s. Over the next 20 years, they discovered its remarkable secrets.

A drain runs past a well and a wall in Mohenjo-Daro.

## Mystery File:
### WASHED AWAY

Why were the Indus Valley cities abandoned? It was probably because they were hit by floods. Around the 1700s B.C., Mohenjo-Daro was flooded by both the Indus River and the Arabian Sea. It never recovered.

When archaeologists dug into the mound, they found the remains of one of the world's oldest cities. It had been buried 5,500 years before. It was a capital of the civilization of the Indus Valley. The walls of another city called Harappa were nearby.

## Ancient Cities

Mohenjo-Daro was built about 3500 B.C. around a strong **citadel**. The streets were laid out in a grid. Many of the homes had an upper floor with brick stairs. The citizens of Mohenjo-Daro even had plumbing. The houses had their own bathrooms with drains.

*Seal from Mohenjo-Daro*

## Mystery words...

**citadel:** a strong fortification used for ruling a city

# The City of MUD

Babylon was one of the most famous ancient cities. It was said to be home to the Tower of Babel, which is mentioned in the Bible. It was also home to one of the Wonders of the World—the famous Hanging Gardens.

Babylon reached a peak of success under King Nebuchadrezzar II (605–561 B.C.). By then, the city had been the capital of Mesopotamia (present-day Iraq) for 3,000 years. It was also a trade center. But for some reason Babylon lost power and was abandoned. Its bricks crumbled into the ground.

A priest directs workers that are building the tower.

## Brilliant City

Nebuchadrezzar expanded the city on the banks of the River Euphrates. He built a great temple to a god named Marduk. Part of the temple was a stepped pyramid called a **ziggurat**. The pyramid might have been the basis for stories of the Tower of Babel, which was said to reach up to heaven.

Babylon's other famous construction was the Hanging Gardens. No-one knows what these ancient gardens looked like, but they amazed everyone who saw them.

## Mystery File:
### HANGING GARDENS

Nebuchadrezzar may have built the gardens for his wife who missed the greenery of her homeland. The gardens had **terraces** and an irrigation system. They may have stood on a rooftop. All that remains today is a mound.

## Mystery words...

ziggurat: a form of pyramid built in a series of steps

# Homer's TROY

In the 7th or 8th century **B.C.**, the ancient **G**reek poet **H**omer described the destruction of the great city of Troy in his **epic** poem "The Iliad." But did the story have any truth in it? Was there a real Troy?

The poem "The Iliad" was popular for many centuries, but no one was sure its story was real. Then, in 1822, a British historian named Charles Maclaren suggested a likely site of Troy. He identified an **earthen** mound near the coast of what is now Turkey. Local people called the place Hisarlik. Fifty years later, a German archaeologist, Heinrich Schliemann, confirmed that Maclaren was right.

*Homer said the Greeks used a wooden horse to overthrow Troy.*

Experts compared the ruins to Homer's poems. One part of the city wall was very weak, as Homer had said about Troy. The city once stood on the coast, as Homer described. Everything matched. Archaeologists decided this was indeed Troy.

## Layer Upon Layer

Schliemann and other experts found that nine cities had been built on the same site. As each city was abandoned, a new city was built on top. Homer's Troy was one of the oldest cities. It had a citadel and large houses. The walls had been destroyed by fire—just as Homer had described in his poem.

*Nine cities stood on the same site over thousands of years.*

Mystery words...

**earthen:** describes something made out of earth

# The Buried ARMY

In 1974, farmers in Xian, China, discovered a 2,000-year-old tomb. The huge underground tomb covered 20 square miles (50 square km). It included an army of thousands of clay warriors.

The tomb belonged to China's first emperor, Qin Shi Huangdi. In the third century B.C., he united China and built the Great Wall to protect the country from invaders from the northwest.

The emperor was terrified of death. He asked priests to find the secret of eternal life. He also built a vast, complex underground tomb to protect him in his next life.

*The warriors are arranged in neat lines, like a parade.*

## Army of Clay

The emperor ordered 700,000 men to build his tomb. They also spent 36 years making 8,000 lifesized warriors out of **terracotta**. No two warriors are alike. As well as warriors, there were chariots, animals, and everything that was needed to protect the emperor in the next world.

Mystery File:
### EMPEROR'S TOMB

Despite finding the terracotta army, archaeologists found no sign of the emperor. They think a nearby mound might be his tomb. They haven't excavated it because it is said to contain mercury, which is poisonous.

Mystery words...

**terracotta:** a kind of clay used for pottery and sculpture

# Victims of the
# VOLCANO

In 1748, a military engineer began to dig at a site near Vesuvius, a volcano near Naples, Italy. The site was known as Civita—"the city." It was soon clear why. The earth fell away to reveal a city buried 1,700 years earlier.

Vesuvius still rises above Pompeii, the city it destroyed.

The city is now the most famous Roman city in the world—Pompeii. It was home to up to 20,000 people when Vesuvius **erupted** on August 24, 79 A.D. Many people fled, but thousands more were trapped as ash rained down, burying the town to a depth of 23 feet (7 m).

## Sealed In

Pompeii and Herculaneum, its neighbor, were completely buried. When they were rediscovered, they were perfectly preserved. Experts even found the shapes of people who had died as they tried to escape.

## Mystery File: PERFECT RECORD

The ash preserved the cities perfectly. The paintings on the walls looked new. There were grapes in a bowl and even bread in the baker's oven. Where people had died, they left holes in the ash. Archaeologists made **casts** of their bodies.

Mystery words...

**casts:** objects made by pouring liquid into molds to harden

# City of the ROCKS

Petra could only be reached through a long, twisting gorge.

The landscape of southwest Jordan is bare rocks, with cliffs and ravines. It seems empty. But in 1812, the German traveler Johann Burckhardt followed his Bedouin guides along the twisting mile-long canyon of the **Wadi Al-Siq**. He was astonished to find the remains of a secret city, carved into the rose-pink rocks.

Mystery words...

wadi: a dry riverbed in the desert, often used as a road

This was Petra. From the sixth century B.C. to the second century A.D., it was a key point on the trade routes between Asia and Europe. The Nabataeans who lived there were very wealthy. They carved buildings and tombs out of the sandstone cliffs.

## Declining Fortunes

Petra was a natural fortress. It was hidden in the cliffs and had a good water supply. But in the end, the city had no defense against changing trade routes. It became isolated and abandoned, but never fully forgotten.

## Mystery File: BUILT IN ROCK

The Nabataeans were not the only people to carve buildings in rock. Lalibela, in Ethiopia, has rock-carved churches. Carving into hills was easier than cutting blocks of rock for building.

Many of the carved buildings in Petra were used as tombs.

# Faces in the
# JUNGLE

For the French archaeologist Henri Mouhot, it was a remarkable discovery. In the middle of the jungle he suddenly found himself looking at huge stone faces smiling at him.

It was 1860. Mouhot was exploring Cambodia, in Southeast Asia. The huge stone faces were carved on a ruined temple in the jungle.

Nearby was another temple. And another. At the heart of the ruined city was the biggest temple of all—Angkor Wat.

## Religious City

Local people did not know who had built the city. In fact, it was their ancestors. The Khmer people built the city of Angkor between 800 and 1400 A.D. Each new king built his own temple. Some were **Buddhist**; others were **Hindu**. When the Khmers lost power, they abandoned their holy city and the jungle grew slowly over the ruins.

## Mystery File:
### ABANDONED CITY

In 1431, Angkor was invaded by its neighbors from Ayutthaya. They removed many treasures from the temples. Khmer power declined; so did the state religion. Most of the temples were abandoned. Angkor fell into ruins.

## Mystery words...

wat: a name for a Buddhist temple in Cambodia and Thailand

# Lost City of the INCA

When the U.S. explorer Hiram Bingham climbed a mountain in Peru in 1912, he found two brothers farming at the top. They were surrounded by the ruins of a stone city that clung to terraces on the steep hillsides.

Bingham had traveled up a river valley near Cusco. Cusco was the capital of the Inca, who had ruled a large **empire** in the Andes in the 15th century A.D. When the Inca were overthrown by the Spaniards in 1532, they continued to live in cities hidden in the mountains. Bingham had found Machu Picchu, one of the "lost" cities of the Inca.

Machu Picchu did not seem like a normal city, however. There was not much room there for people to live. It may have had a special purpose. Perhaps it was a royal palace. Or perhaps it had a religious purpose.

Mystery words...

empire: a group of states with a single ruler, or emperor

## Mystery File:
## SUN WORSHIP

The city has a short stone column called a hitching post. It lines up with nearby peaks. Inca priests performed rituals there to "tie" the Sun to the Earth. It is thought this was to ensure the Sun came back each spring.

*The city stood among high mountain peaks.*

23

# Africa's Royal CITY

In Zimbabwe, in southern Africa, most buildings are huts of mud and wood. But large stone walls on the plains mark the site of a lost city. It was once home to up to 20,000 people.

The ruins of the city cover an area of 200 acres (80 ha).

The "stone houses" are the remains of Great Zimbabwe. The Shona people lived here from the 11th to the 15th century. They raised cattle, grew crops, and traded gold. Their wealth was reflected in fine stone buildings. But then the city was abandoned for reasons we do not know.

# Mystery File:
## GREAT ENCLOSURE

At the heart of Great Zimbabwe was the Great Enclosure. It was the largest structure in southern Africa. It was a **conical** tower surrounded by **two tall circular stone walls.** The tower may have been the **religious** center of the city.

## Mystery Origin

European explorers discovered the ruins of Great Zimbabwe in the 19th century. They were amazed by the sophisticated building techniques they found. That led them to conclude that an early European civilization must have built the city. Some people suggested the ancient Greeks had built it. It was not until the 20th century that archaeologists were finally able to prove that the city was built by Africans.

## Mystery words...

**conical:** in the shape of a cone that tapers to a blunt point

# Pakal's Resting PLACE

The ruins in the tropical forests of southern Mexico were never fully lost. People began to explore these forests in the 19th century. In the mid-20th century some of jungle was cleared and magnificent pyramids and palaces were revealed. Virtually all of the city still remains hidden in the thick foliage.

Pakal's tomb lay beneath the Temple of Inscriptions (left).

For around 300 years, from 600–900 A.D., Palenque was an important city of the Mayans who ruled Mexico and Guatemala. The city's wealth was reflected in the high-quality of the carvings on its buildings.

## Magnificent City

Most of the best buildings were constructed during the reign of Pakal the Great, from 615 to 683. The city had remarkable palaces, pyramids, and **aqueducts** to carry water. Palenque was abandoned near the end of the 10th century. The Maya probably fled after the city was invaded by enemies.

This carving shows Pakal in an elaborate royal headdress.

## Mystery File:

### PAKAL THE GREAT

Inscriptions name Pakal as the main builder of Palenque. In 1952, archaeologist Alberto Ruiz Lhuillier found the king's tomb buried beneath the Temple of Inscriptions. Pakal's remains were covered in rich jade ornaments.

Mystery words...

inscriptions: words carved into stone as a permanent record

# City of the GODS

When the Aztecs rose to power in Mexico, a ruined city of pyramids already stood there. The Aztecs believed the universe was created there. They called the site Teotihuacan, or "birthplace of the gods."

At the heart of the city, a broad avenue linked the two largest pyramids, known as the Pyramid of the Sun and the Pyramid of the Moon. Smaller pyramids lined the avenue. The Aztecs called the street the Avenue of the Dead. They made religious **pilgrimages** to the site. They were certain that this was where their own gods had created the Sun.

Mystery words...

pilgrimages: journeys to a sacred place or a shrine

## Mexican City

Teotihuacan was actually built by an unknown people from Mexico in the first century B.C. When it was abandoned around 500 A.D., it had about 200,000 citizens and was bigger than Rome. It covered an area of 8 square miles (20 square km). The city probably fell when civil war broke out among its rulers.

The Pyramid of the Sun towers over the Avenue of the Dead.

## Mystery File:
### HUMAN SACRIFICE

In 2004, human skeletons were found beneath the Pyramid of the Moon. Were the people killed during the building process? Some early cultures in Mexico believed that human sacrifice was necessary to keep the gods happy.

# Glossary

**anarchy** A time when there is no law and order

**aqueducts** Artificial channels for carrying water

**archaeologist** Someone who studies objects from the past

**Buddhist** Someone who follows the religious teachings of the Buddha

**casts** Objects made by pouring liquid into molds to harden

**citadel** A strong fortification used for ruling a city

**conical** Having the shape of a cone that tapers to a blunt point

**earthen** Describes something made out of earth

**empire** A group of states with a single ruler, or emperor

**epic** A long poem about heroic deeds

**erupted** Exploded with great force

**Hindu** Someone who follows an ancient religion from India

**inscriptions** Words carved into stone as a permanent record

**pilgrimage** Journeys to a sacred place or shrine

**sonar** A system that locates objects by bouncing sound waves off them

**terraces** Flat steps cut into the side of a hill

**terracotta** A kind of clay used for pottery and sculpture

**wadi** The dry course of a river in the desert, often used as a road

**wat** A name for a Buddhist temple in Cambodia and Thailand

**ziggurat** A form of pyramid built in a series of steps

# Find Out More

## BOOKS

Clements, Gillian. *Indus Valley City* (Building History). Sea to Sea Publications, 2009.

Kerns, Ann. *Troy* (Unearthing Ancient Worlds). Twenty-First Century Books, 2008.

Morris, Neil. *Lost Cities* (Amazing History). Smart Apple Media, 2008.

Price, Sean Stewart. *Kids' Guide to Lost Cities* (Edge Books). Capstone Press, 2011.

Rinaldo, Denise. *Cities of the Dead: Finding Lost Civilizations* (24/7: Science Behind the Scenes: Mystery Files). Children's Press, 2008.

Weill, Ann. *The World's Most Amazing Lost Cities* (Raintree Perspectives). Heinemann-Raintree, 2011.

## WEBSITES

National Geographic gallery of photographs of lost cities.
*http://science.nationalgeographic.com/science/archaeology/photos/lost-cities/*

Listverse.com list of the Top 10 lost cities.
*http://listverse.com/2011/09/09/top-10-lost-cities/*

Discovery.com guide to the continuing search for lost cities.
*http://news.discovery.com/earth/lost-cities-120618.html*

How Stuff Works pages about five important lost cities.
*http://adventure.howstuffworks.com/5-lost-cities.htm*

# Index

Africa, southern 24–25
Andes Mountains 22
Angkor 20–21
archaeologists 9, 13, 15,
    17, 25, 27
Atlantic Ocean 6, 7
Atlantis 6–7
Avenue of the Dead 28
Aztec 28

Babylon 4, 10–11
Bingham, Hiram 22
Buddhism 21
Burckhardt, Johann 18

Cambodia 20–21
China 14–15
Cusco 22

Ethiopia 19

Great Enclosure 25
Great Wall 14
Great Zimbabwe 24–25
Greece, ancient 6, 7,
    12–13, 25
Guatemala 27

Hanging Gardens 10, 11
Harappa 9
Herculaneum 17
Hinduism 21

Hisarlik 12
Homer 12–13
human sacrifice 29

Illiad 12, 13
Inca 22–23
Indus Valley 8–9
Italy 16–17

Jordan 18–19
jungle 20–21, 26

Khmer empire 21

Lalibela 19
Lhuillier, Alberto Ruiz 27

Machu Picchu 22–23
Maclaren, Charles 12
Mayans 27
Mesopotamia 10–11
Mexico 26–27, 28–29
Mohenjo-Daro 8–9
Mouhot, Henri 20

Nabataeans 19
Nebuchadrezzar II 10, 11

Pakal 26–27
Pakistan 8–9
Palenque 26–27
Peru 22–23

Petra 5, 18–19
Pompeii 4, 16–17
Pyramid of the Moon 29
Pyramid of the Sun 28, 29
pyramids 7, 28, 29

Qin Shi Huangdi 14–15

rock buildings 19
Rome, ancient 16–17

Schliemann, Heinrich 12,
    13
Shona (people) 24

Temple of Inscriptions 26,
    27
Teotihuacan 28–29
terracotta armies 15
Tower of Babel 10, 11
Troy 12–13
Turkey 12

Vesuvius 16, 17
volcanoes 16, 17

Xian 14

ziggurat 10, 11
Zimbabwe 24–25